An Hachette UK Company
www.hachette.co.uk

First published in Great Britain in 2018 by Hamlyn,
an imprint of Octopus Publishing Group Ltd, Carmelite House,
50 Victoria Embankment, London EC4Y 0DZ
www.octopusbooks.co.uk

Cartoons

British Cartoon Archive

Cartoons supplied by British Cartoon Archive
Cartoons compiled by John Field

ISBN 978 0 60063 475 1

A CIP catalogue record for this book is available from the British Library.

Printed and bound in China

1 3 5 7 9 10 8 6 4 2

The Collection
2019

compiled by John Field

EXPRESS NEWSPAPERS

hamlyn

Contents

Introduction: On This Day

Giles commented on the world, in his individual and inimitable style, three or four times a week for almost half a century. He saw great humour in a wide range of situations and captured much of it in his cartoons. This collection takes us month-by-month through the year and covers many important events which have occurred in both the life of the UK and internationally.

Occasionally, Giles liked to use the coincidence of two unrelated events, linked only by time and theme, to form the basis of his humour. Such as on 1 August 1963, when he linked two national sex scandals. Another cartoon, 30 July 1970, links the end of the traditional Royal Navy daily ration of rum with the drafting of sailors for land-based activities, unloading ships, due to a dock strike.

Another joke he enjoyed was contrasting an important event with a relatively ordinary, or even insignificant, item. See 24 July 1967, which links the first landing and walking on the moon with the naming of a child. On 27 August 1980, he contrasted violent rioting in Hong Kong with a tranquil English garden scene, while on 23 September 1986, a crucial peace conference is connected to a school choir practice. On 7 April 1960, an important official visit to London by the President of France is linked with a cockney's annoyance about the government's recent increase in tax on the price of cigarettes (it should be noted that Giles was a heavy smoker).

It is also obvious from his cartoons that Giles enjoyed picking up on British regional preoccupations, such as the Loch Ness Monster, impossibly-long Welsh place names, frugal Scots and the Lancashire–Yorkshire feud: the latter illustrated here on 18 February 1971. More difficult aspects of British life are also represented in this collection. Cartoons relating to strike action appear on 6 December 1953 (engineers), 3 August 1972 (dock workers), 18 January 1979 (rail workers) and 7 February 1988 (seamen).

On another note, Giles frequently used his cartoons to mark important national events such as Charles and Diana's wedding at St Paul's Cathedral (26 July 1981) and the Notting Hill Carnival (26 August 1980). Other national phenomena, such as the Great Train Robbery (15 August 1963), Beatlemania (29 October 1963) and Billy Graham's Christian crusade (18 March 1954) are all recorded in his work.

Turning to the international stage, one subject frequently covered was the Cold War and the associated Space Race between the USA and the USSR. The cartoon dated 27 December 1957 portrays an extremely worrying proliferation of nuclear weapons on both sides, while three cartoons represent the Space Race: 4 February 1958 (first dog in space), 10 August 1961 (Russia's manned spacecraft) and 10 June 1965 (the Americans achieving the first walk in space).

Keeping on the international theme, a number of cartoons cover diplomatic and state issues including an important conference between the then "Big Four" – UK, USA, USSR and France (26 January 1954), another summit meeting of the "Big Four" in Paris (15 May 1960) and an International Conference on Palestine (24 June 1980). The cartoon dated 25 November 1956, relates to the Suez Crisis and that on 11 May 1967 is concerned with the Greek Military Junta. Summing it all up, the 25 April 1961 cartoon aptly draws attention to increasingly widespread turmoil being experienced around the world.

In addition to addressing worldwide events, Giles, of course, covered many subjects particularly dear to the British: sport, pubs, the weather, grumbling about rail transport, the cost of food, strikes, politicians, landladies, traffic wardens and many more. One cannot help but feel that, sometimes, Giles used the cartoons to air his own thoughts on some of these subjects.

The craze for "streaking" at various sporting events was covered on 14 March 1974 and even political party conferences are included (9 October 1966). Being a farmer himself, a large number of Giles's cartoons relate to the farming world and it is represented here by a cartoon referring to the Smithfield Agricultural Show (5 December 1961).

Regarding sport, while cricket (9 July 1961), tennis (21 June 1956), sailing (18 September 1958), the Olympics (3 September 1972) and car rallies (11 November 1953) are all included in this collection, Giles reserves special attention for football. A keen supporter of Ipswich Town Football Club, he intensely disliked the growth of hooliganism in the sport. During his drawing career, he produced a number of cartoons exposing it and two are included here: 22 April 1975 and 19 August 1984. His work also illustrates his displeasure with street riots and violence generally: 20 May 1969 relates to an unpleasant fight between mods and rockers in Folkestone while 17 August 1977 shows the result of violent rioting by the National Front.

The great British pub was always close to Giles's heart, and he even had a pub in Islington named after him, The Giles Pub (Giles is pictured with the landlord and landlady, see above right). The country's many public houses make a number of appearances

including 9 June 1959, which introduced new opening hours for pubs, and 11 February 1982, chronicling a law allowing children into pubs, something of which I doubt Giles approved.

I hope that this collection adequately illustrates not only the very broad scope of Giles's work but also his humanity as a man prepared to see the best in people, his ability to see fun and laughter wherever possible, and his readiness to make a serious statement where required.

The Grandma Sisterhood Saga (continued)

Readers of recent editions will be aware of my growing concern about the proliferation of Grandma's sisters at large in Giles's world. To quickly recap, in addition to Grandma herself, there is cartoon proof that two live "up North", one near Aberystwyth, one is in Aberdeen, one in Ireland, one (named Ivy) was identified in the 2017 collection, and another (named Florrie) was discovered in last year's collection. In addition, there is potentially an unspecified number in Australia as a result of Grandma's father's time at Botany Bay, but we can only hope that this is not the case.

Since last year, two further sightings have been made and both are included in this collection. The first is on 23 December 1972, when Auntie Vi arrived at Ipswich station for Christmas (see below). I have no doubt that she is Grandma's sister – just look at her!

The second sighting is in the cartoon from 11 March 1973, with an Aunt Millie arriving at the Giles' family home in a hot air balloon for Sunday lunch. The figure is too small to be certain but she appears to be waving a Grandma-type handbag. I am prepared to venture that any elderly lady choosing that form of transport in order to have a free lunch is almost certainly closely related to Grandma.

One final point – following publication of last year's collection, a kind reader has brought to my attention the cartoon on the cover of the 43rd series of Giles cartoons (see page 160). It clearly shows a Grandma sister with a label on her handbag saying "Cork", which definitely confirms, I am afraid, the existence of one of the breed living across the Irish Sea.

This makes a total of ten sisters (including Grandma) in the Northern Hemisphere and perhaps an unknown number in the Southern. It is just possible, however, that some of those we have been unable to name are, in fact, those referred to as living in Scotland, Wales, Ireland or "up North". So there may be an element of double-counting – we can only hope so!

John Field

January

The Coal Industry Nationalisation Act came into force five days earlier bringing into government ownership 958 colleries previously owned by around 800 companies.

"We know it's YOUR mine and all that – but the management would prefer fewer of these family inspections."

Sunday Express, 5 January 1947

The USA was becoming increasingly influential in the Middle East – not always popular with the Old Guard – see the paintings on the wall.

"But, Sir, surely you bought your Empire for a few strings of beads."

Daily Express, 8 January 1957

Three days earlier, Giles's football team, Ipswich Town, had been beaten 3–2 by Peterborough in the third round of the FA Cup. At this time, many thousands of US airmen were stationed in Suffolk but research can find no evidence of an accident involving A-bombs. The name of the pub in the distance is a combination of the names of the two Ipswich breweries at that time – Tolly's and Cobbolds.

"I suppose what with us dumping A-bombs on 'em and their Town team getting knocked out of the Cup ..."

Daily Express, 12 January 1960

Records show that after a relatively mild spell, temperatures fell sharply two days before this cartoon appeared, with up to 12 inches of snow in some parts of Southern England. As usual, it was anticipated that this would cause the normal total disruption of life in Britain under such circumstances but, in fact, the weather picked up within a few days.

"Progress is the realisation of Utopias." (Oscar Wilde)

Daily Express, 14 January 1964

This was a period which became known as the "Winter of Discontent" in Britain with widespread public sector strikes over wages.

"May my first case of the day be a rail striker – six years minimum!"

Daily Express, 18 January 1979

A period of intense discord in the British Government about the British helicopter manufacturer, Westland, concerning its future merger with a European company or Sikorsky, an American company. Both Michael Heseltine, the Defence Minister, and the Trade and Industry Secretary, Leon Brittan, resigned as a result of the debate, with the British Government eventually accepting the US link.

"Michael, Leon, Westland, Sikorsky – I appreciate they were the first sounds she uttered, but aren't they rather odd names to call a girl?"

Sunday Express, 19 January 1986

The previous year, at the start of the Falklands War, the Prime Minister Margaret Thatcher, had told Parliament,
"The people of the Falkland Islands shall be free to determine their own way of life and their own future.
The wishes of the Islanders must be paramount".

"I appreciate the Islanders' wishes are paramount...I simply said I wish it wasn't me who makes bloody sure they are."

Daily Express, 20 January 1983

The first passenger-carrying jumbo jet, a boeing 747, arrived in London on this day – with 324 passengers (Giles must have estimated that the crew will have drunk at least 26 gins etc. or some passengers demanded seconds). The flight from New York to Heathrow was, unfortunately, seven hours late due to technical problems.

"There they go, 350 Jumbo gins, 350 Jumbo tonics, 350...."

Daily Express, 22 January 1970

18 In the UK, it became an offence to drive, attempt to drive or be in charge of a motor vehicle on a road or other public place while "unfit to drive through drink or drugs".

"This one's the BREATHALYZER, sir – that one's a sergeant."

Sunday Express, 24 January 1960

Four days earlier saw the first commercial flights of the Anglo–French supersonic airliner – the Concorde. Simultaneously, at 11.40am, two aircraft took off, one from London bound for Bahrain and the other from Paris flying to Rio de Janeiro via Dakar in Senegal.

"They give a wonderful description of their first earth-shrinking Concorde trip, considering they were both sound asleep from Heathrow to Bahrain."

Sunday Express, 25 January 1976

Although there was some hope of a "thaw" in East–West relations at the Berlin Conference, little progress was made. However, the Soviets did agree to withdraw from Austria if it was made neutral.

"Boy Tom and Boy Dick be discussing Berlin Peace Conference."

Daily Express, 26 January 1954

Malta was granted independence from the UK in September 1964 but British military bases remained on the island until March 1979 after a period of gradual withdrawal.

"There's your first international repercussion for calling home the troops – Maria says no more tick."

Daily Express, 31 January 1967

February

The announcement that women may now study at Oxford in unlimited numbers was welcomed by most male undergrads. "But," said a well-known warden to a don, "kindly explain to little Miss Whatsit that such studies as boat racing, the placing of utensils on spires, debagging of Principals, were always — and shall remain — the undisputed privileges of the Male."

Daily Express, 1 February 1957

On 3 November 1957, three months before this cartoon appeared, the Russians had launched a space craft with Laika, a dog, aboard. It was another important step in the Space Race but, unfortunately, Laika did not survive. Presumably the Russians did not announce the flight immediately. The cartoon picks up the point that the British are considered a nation of dog lovers.

"Ma'am, to my knowledge we ain't sent a dog up in ours, but if we ever do may I be to hell and gone from these islands."

Daily Express, 4 February 1958

24

A week earlier, thousands of seamen had gone on strike over pay and on 4 February, despite the National Union of Seamen backing down in the High Court and calling an end to the strike action, defiant seamen continued to strike for several more weeks.

"Your wife won't be happy in the new house – you taking the wrong road with the furniture and spending the weekend down here."

Sunday Express, 7 February 1988

Two weeks earlier, General Charles de Gaulle, President of France, vetoed the UK's application to join the European Economic Community.

"Agreed then — we send a note to de Gaulle telling him if he don't like Britain this club is cancelling its annual day-trip to Boulogne."

Sunday Express, 10 February 1963

The law was changed at this time to allow children under the age of 16 to enter a public house if accompanied by an adult.

"Get him off my chair."

Daily Express, 11 February 1982

The 1974 General Election was held two weeks later and won by Labour under Harold Wilson. In the run-up to the election various proposals appeared in the party manifestos to help the agricultural industry. This coincided with a period of unrest regarding farm labourers' wages.

"Right! Which one's the cupid?"

Daily Express, 14 February 1974

28   Due to financial constraints, the government had just announced that spending on the Royal Navy would go ahead but at a reduced level. See also the Army's reaction to a similar situation 12 years earlier in cartoon dated 21 February 1954.

"I wouldn't say the Royal Navy Club was the best place for a Flight Lieutenant to mention the Navy being as dead as a dodo."

Daily Express, 15 February 1966

The Local Government Boundary Commission was the body established to settle the boundaries, names and electoral arrangements of Local Authorities for changes to be implemented in 1974. This was one of the trickier problems for them to solve concerning two strong-minded counties.

"Art thou trying to start another War of t'bloody Roses, Mr. Walker? Your new Yorkshire–Lancashire boundary goes right through my parlour."

Daily Express, 18 February 1971

30 The British Government had announced that it was to test nuclear bombs in Australia and over the next five years, 12 major tests were conducted. These tests were mostly done at surface level and took place at Montebello Islands, Emu Field and Maralinga.

"O.K., you just keep playing around out there – you'll soon see why it's better to stay indoors."

Daily Express, 19 February 1952

The pictures on the wall help to explain the "Old Man's" likely reaction.

31

"You'll know all about atomic explosions and guided missiles when the Old Man comes to the page about the Army being placed second to the Air Force."

Daily Express, 21 February 1954

32 Due to food shortages, both during the War and in the period of austerity that followed, rationing continued for many years with meat rationing not ending until nine years after the end of hostilities.

"And for the first time in thirteen years I expect I'll have to buy me own beer."

Sunday Express, 22 February 1953

This was the time of a major blockade by French lorry drivers affecting the whole of France with about 240 road blocks around the country. It was estimated that it left almost 300 British lorry drivers trapped in France.

"I'll give him just a couple of days of this: 'Madame Francoise didn't cook it like this in Lyons during the Great Blockade'."

Sunday Express, 26 February 1984

Giles has picked up on the coincidence of a period of severe flooding in many parts of the country with the success, at that time, of a novel by the author Clive Cussler entitled *Raise the Titanic*.

"Read all about it – Raise the Titanic."

Sunday Express, 27 February 1977

March

This was the Queen's first visit to the West Coast in the USA. The trip started in San Diego and continued up the coast, visiting Los Angeles, San Francisco and Seattle, and then on to Victoria, British Columbia in Canada.

"The Brits bought Manhattan for half what you just paid for that flag."

Daily Express, 1 March 1983

At that time, the Royal Society had just reported its concern about the emigration of scientists from this country, primarily to the USA, and sparked the phrase "Brain Drain".

"If the Americans are over here buying all our scientific talent how come they missed you?"

Sunday Express, 3 March 1963

British Prime Minister, James Callaghan, had flown to Washington, D.C. on a Concorde aircraft for a series of meetings with the recently elected US President, Jimmy Carter. This was a period when Britain was suffering severe financial constraints.

"My brother-in-law in the British Police cabled me: 'Don't expect no gratuities'."

Daily Express, 9 March 1977

The Associated Society of Locomotive Engineers and Firemen had announced a series of one-day strikes on Sundays in response to proposals to re-structure train drivers' pay.

"Come rail strikes, hell and high water – nothing will stop your Aunt Millie getting here for lunch on Sunday."

Sunday Express, 11 March 1973

This was a period when streaking, particularly at sporting events, had become a craze.

"Come off it, Harry. Bringing back hanging as a deterrent to Streaking is a bit thick."

Daily Express, 14 March 1974

Various forms of boycott had become a tool in industrial disputes in Britain at this time.

"They're giving me the old 'Angry Silence'."

Daily Express, 15 March 1960

This was a period of increasing petrol prices due in part to tax increases.

41

"Don't book me for calling him a cheat ... I called him a bloody thief."

Daily Express, 17 March 1981

Billy Graham, an American evangelist was in Britain on a religious "crusade" and spoke to enormous crowds at Wembley Stadium. Part of his message certainly got through to Grandma.

"Mr. Billy Graham has told America that one in four first-born Britons are born out of wedlock, so Grandma insists that we find her birth certificate."

Daily Express, 18 March 1954

The long-running miners' strike was a major industrial action which shut down the British coal industry in an attempt by the miners to prevent colliery closures. It started two weeks before this cartoon and continued until March the following year. Note the similarity between this police sergeant and the one in cartoon dated 26 August 1980 – no doubt he was known to Giles as he appears in a number of cartoons.

"By the way, while you were away keeping order at the pits, someone nicked all our coal."

Daily Express, 20 March 1984

44   Three days earlier, the first walk in space was undertaken by Russian astronaut, Alexei Leonov. It took place during the period of a race for supremacy in space between the USA and the USSR and was considered a coup for the Soviet Union.

"Mother's very cross with you all for hanging baby out of the window on a wire to see if he can walk in space."

Daily Express, 21 March 1965

At the British Government's invitation, a group of high-ranking Russians visited Britain from 18–27 March. They were received by the Queen at Windsor Castle, had discussions with the Prime Minister at Downing Street and Chequers and visited the Houses of Parliament. The visit also included visits to Edinburgh, Birmingham and Oxford.

"Malik, Malenkov, Serov, Krushchev, Bulganin – if them Russians was to declare war today there'd be half of 'em over here already."

Sunday Express, 25 March 1956

The Lincoln Handicap (see Dad's newspaper) is traditionally the first race of the Flat Racing season. It was relocated from Lincoln three years after this cartoon appeared and is now run at Doncaster Racecourse.

"You're out of his reach — ask him how went the Sort of Kings, yesterday."

Daily Express, 27 March 1962

April

The UK joined the European Economic Community on 1 January that year and as a consequence,
Purchase Tax was replaced by Value Added Tax on 1 April.

"I know I haven't got the hang of it yet – she's just charged me VAT."

Daily Express, 3 April 1973

General de Gaulle was on a state visit to London. Three days earlier the government had announced a 2d. price increase on cigarettes in the budget.

"Reckon he heard you say if they did away with a few Horse Guards they'd have saved that extra 2d. on your fags."

Daily Express, 7 April 1960

Gorbachev was on a two-day goodwill visit to the UK where he had detailed discussions with the Prime Minister, Margaret Thatcher. He expressed the desire, as part of Glasnost, to remake his country into part of what he called the "Common European House".

"I know they love Gorbachev but I'm not having vodka and balalaika all day."

The teachers were demonstrating over pay disputes.

"If any of them shouted at me like they shouted at the Minister of Education I'd annihilate 'em."

Daily Express, 10 April 1980

The summer of 1976 became known as the "Drought of the Century" with high temperatures and hardly any rainfall requiring the introduction of a hosepipe ban in some areas of the country.

"Think very carefully, sonny — are you absolutely sure that was the man you saw using a hose on his window box?"

Sunday Express, 11 April 1976

52 A replica of the seventeenth-century *Mayflower* sailed across the Atlantic, leaving Plymouth, Devon on 20 April that year and arriving in New York on 1 July. Perhaps the traditional spring cleaning exercise made father think that the pilgrims going off to the New World to find a new life was not a bad idea.

"Why's Dad trying to book a single reservation on the Mayflower?"

Sunday Express, 14 April 1957

Uncle Rodney's memoirs will relate to a naval engagement which took place almost 70 years earlier off the Falkland Islands, in December 1914 between the Royal Navy and the German Imperial Navy. All but one of the German vessels involved were sunk. As a consequence, Germany's only permanent overseas naval formation – the German East Asia Squadron – ceased to exist. Presumably the British action against the Argentinians at this time brought back memories for him.

"Uncle Rodney's getting in early with his memoirs of the Battle of the Falklands."

Sunday Express, 18 April 1982

The armed services had just received a substantial pay rise.

"Git up there, you 'orrible fat little capitalist beasts! Let's be earning our 24.2% rise!"

Daily Express, 19 April 1979

Bessie Braddock was Member of Parliament for Liverpool Exchange from 1945 until 1970. She was a formidable character with a strong outspoken approach to life as a politician.

"You did that deliberately, Bessie Braddock! Just to ruin my TV image"

Daily Express, 21 April 1966

A period of football hooliganism in our country – something which Giles, being a true football supporter, detested.

"That's the bail for your son, Madam, now what about the bail for your husband?"

Daily Express, 22 April 1975

The next day, Princess Alexandra and Angus Ogilvy married at Westminster Abbey.

57

"That's my Bertie – always with the romance. Reckons he could do Kensington Palace to Westminster in 3½ minutes dead with the roads cleared"

Daily Express, 23 April 1963

58 This was a very tense period in many parts of the world with hostilities building up in Vietnam, the Bay of Pigs invasion in Cuba a week earlier, and unrest elsewhere including Guatemala and the Congo. France was in turmoil over Algeria's fight for independence.

"Oddly enough, one of the few places we could have gone where they're not having a revolution at the moment is the USSR."

Daily Express, 25 April 1961

A few months previously, Field Marshal Montgomery had published his memoirs which caused considerable offence, particularly in the USA. He then went on a goodwill tour to the Soviet Union where he spoke of the absurdity of two great power blocs spending vast resources on armaments that neither wished to use against the other.

"Mummy – be a dear and stop boiling the kettle on Tex's head."

Daily Express, 30 April 1959

May

On 12 January 1976, Prince Charles was appointed to the Royal Navy minehunter *HMS Bronington* and on 9 February he took command of her. He relinquished his command on 15 December that year – the final day of his active service in the Royal Navy.

"Prince Charles says he's aged ten years in four months on his ship. It only takes a weekend on ours."

Sunday Express, 2 May 1976

"For the crazy British – they take them like so and throw them all over the pitch – don't aska me why."

Daily Express, 5 May 1970

The British steel industry, having been nationalised in February 1951 under Clement Attlee's Labour Government, was almost totally de-nationalised by the later Conservative Government by July 1957. However, the new Labour Government under Harold Wilson, elected in October 1964, announced, at the time of this cartoon, its intention to re-nationalise the industry but this did not take place until 1967, so the worker's takeover bid was a little premature.

"Get this, Milligan! Nationalisation isn't going to mean all men in the steel industry are equal by a damn long chalk."

Daily Express, 6 May 1965

A rail strike at this time became a very grave situation and it was reported that stones were being thrown at trains, boulders being placed on the tracks and rails being tampered with. On occasions, locomotives had to be manned by rail supervisory staff to keep some services running.

"I'd rather get a rocket from the N.U.R. for not striking when they say 'Strike' than one from her Ladyship for striking when she says 'Don't'."

Daily Express, 9 May 1958

The Greek Military Junta, carried out by a group of far right-wing colonels, took control of the country on April 1967. It lasted until July 1974 and quickly brought in laws aimed at curbing their idea of disreputable behaviour.

Greece has decided not to allow foreigners with beards or long hair into the country. They will also keep out people who are unclean or improperly dressed.

Daily Express, 11 May 1967

A Summit Meeting of the Big Four (UK, USA, USSR and France) was being held in Paris with the aim of reducing Cold War tensions. Unfortunately it was doomed to fail, because two weeks earlier an American U2 spy plane had been shot down over the Soviet Union by a Russian missile after it had lost height through engine trouble – hence Giles's reference to spies.

"That one is American – it whistled."

Sunday Express, 15 May 1960

66   A period of very high inflation with the UK experiencing an average of just over 18 per cent at this time. This pub in Ipswich is one of a number frequented by Giles and was often used by a cycling club. The publican at the time is shown peeping though the window.

"So far she hasn't joined in the chorus of witty jokes about inflation."

Sunday Express, 18 May 1980

A period of street brawls between Mods and Rockers – this time in Folkestone. Two days earlier a Soviet spacecraft, Venera 6, took atmospheric data from the planet Venus which was sent back to Earth.

"Lucky Venus."

Daily Express, 20 May 1969

There had been a telephone bomb scare on the famous ship *QE2*, en route from New York to Southampton, with a ransom note demanding 350,000 US dollars. Giles has located this cartoon at the Felixstowe Ferry Sailing Club, near his farm in Suffolk – he was President of the Club for many years.

"Mind if I check your gear for bombs – some of them in this Club'll do anything to win a race."

Sunday Express, 21 May 1972

This was during the Falklands War which began when General Galtieri, President of Argentina, ordered the invasion of the islands. Within days of the end of the war, Galtieri was removed from power.

"If you'd sent your Grandma on holiday to Buenos Aires two months ago there wouldn't be a Junta now."

Sunday Express, 23 May 1982

70 There was considerable international unrest at this time about the Soviet Union's invasion of Afghanistan, resulting in a threat by a number of countries to boycott the Summer Olympics. Several countries joined the USA in a full boycott but others, including the UK, supported the boycott but left the decision up to individual athletes or the various National Olympic Sports committees.

"Robert is so against sending athletes to Moscow on principle, I wish he would apply his principles to St Botolph's Fete."

Sunday Express, 25 May 1980

This was a period of great civil unrest in France which basically brought the economy of the country to a halt. Students took a strong role in the unrest with enormous demonstrations in the streets of the big cities. The committee here obviously wished to emulate the example given by Emily Davison, who in the 1913 Epsom Derby, threw herself under the hooves of the King's horse in order to bring attention to the fight for votes for women in Britain. She died three days later.

"Drucilla, the committee has decided that you shall have the honour of being thrown in front of Billy Fury's horse at Tattenham Corner."

Daily Express, 28 May 1968

June

This was the first World Cup to be held in North America and the first outside Europe and South America. It was won by Brazil and England was beaten at the Quarter Final stage by West Germany 3–2. The Epsom Derby was run four days after this cartoon appeared and was won by the famous racehorse, Nijinsky, ridden by Lester Piggott.

"I don't think disguising ourselves as natives fools anyone, Ethel. Translated he just called me a feelthy Ingleesh supporter and asked what's going to win tomorrow's Derby."

Daily Express, 2 June 1970

Two days earlier, the wearing of motor cycle helmets became compulsory. However, in November 1941, crash helmets had become compulsory for all British Army motorcyclists when on duty.

"They are not compulsory for all of us — only for those among us with motor cycles."

Sunday Express, 3 June 1973

"They've got an 'Alert' on."

Sunday Express, 5 June 1960

The United Kingdom European Communities Membership referendum, on whether or not to stay in the Common Market, had taken place the day before with the 67.2 per cent of votes in favour of remaining and 32.8 per cent against.

"Of course, he realises we went to the poll for his future, his generation, his security, don't you, little sweetheart?"

Daily Express, 6 June 1975

This was the Silver Jubilee of the Queen's accession to the thrones of the UK and other Commonwealth realms. Street parties were held up and down the country in celebration.

"Ladies! What would her Majesty say – just because you say your neighbour's hung on to three of your chairs and she says you've nicked six of her forks."

Daily Express, 8 June 1977

"It works out nice, Harry. 5 a.m. till 1 p.m., The Bull; 1 p.m. till 9 p.m., The Pig; 9 p.m. till 5 a.m., The Lion."

Daily Express, 9 June 1959

This was at the height of the "Space Race" between the USA and the USSR. One week earlier, the Americans had managed to achieve the first space walk by an astronaut and, no doubt, were waiting to see how the Russians would respond.

"Mr. President? I guess they've sure set the pace this time."

Daily Express, 10 June 1965

The Conservative Party, under Margaret Thatcher, won this election for the third successive time. The musician, Screaming Lord Sutch, was the Founder and Leader of the Official Monster Raving Loony Party for which he unsuccessfully stood for parliamentary election on many occasions.

"In case you've voted for Screaming Lord Sutch – he's not running."

Daily Express, 11 June 1987

This refers to Lawrence Olivier who was awarded an MBE many years earlier.

"I don't recall us kicking up all this dust when Olivier got gonged for playing Hamlet."

Daily Express, 17 June 1965

Dynasty was a hugely popular US TV soap opera in the 1980s, showing a wealthy version of the American way of life. It was based on an oil-rich family living in Denver, Colorado and, no doubt, the nurses were a little disappointed.

"I was thinking more on the lines of hospitals like in Dynasty."

Daily Express, 18 June 1987

Maybe Giles was expressing his own views on two weeks' non-stop tennis on television.

"Come home, Father – and we'll promise we won't have Wimbledon on the radio and television all day long for a fortnight."

Daily Express, 21 June 1956

"Three months Northern Ireland, 11 weeks Falklands, now report for crowd control outside St. Mary's Hospital!"

Daily Express, 22 June 1982

84 This was a conference, held in Venice, of the nine members of the Economic Committee of the European Economic Community, in conjunction with the Palestinian Liberation Organisation. The conference's declaration acknowledged Palestine's right to self-government. At this time, Italy was experiencing political unrest from both left-wing and right-wing groups.

"OK! So I had six Heads of State on board at the same time so I mista the chance!"

Daily Express, 24 June 1980

July

Rationing of various food commodities continued for many years after World War II and meat was still rationed until July 1954.

FOOTNOTE TO A DAILY EXPRESS READER'S LETTER "...people will not pay for what they do not get – real meat. We get bones, gristle, and fat. To cope with the modern idea of meat we must develop fangs of Alsatian dogs."

Daily Express, 3 July 1953

England was playing Australia in the Third Test Match at Headingley, Leeds. England won the match by eight wickets but Australia won the series. This excellent piece of drawing shows Giles's ability to capture both a detailed street scene and the obvious incomprehension of the Italian onlookers.

"Davidson sends down a Chinaman – Subba Row plays it to silly mid-off, through the covers to the boundary for four, but the umpire has signalled 'No ball', etc., etc...."

Sunday Express, 9 July 1961

Twenty-eight-year-old Prince Charles wore First Nation clothes, including a feathered headdress, whilst in Calgary, Alberta on his visit to Canada. He was given the name "Red Crow" as a Chief of the Kanai tribe.

"I trust HRH Red Crow realises that last little ceremonial puff made my daughter the future Queen of England."

Sunday Express, 10 July 1977

In 1965, the death penalty was abolished in Great Britain after a seven-and-a half hour debate in Parliament. Moves to re-introduce the death penalty in certain cases of murder, at the time of this cartoon, were later defeated.

"Let's see if we can find Daddy a category that qualifies him for hanging."

Daily Express, 12 July 1983

"Same with mine – 'your boy swallowing a new ½p. does not constitute an emergency.'"

Daily Express, 16 July 1974

This refers to the military intervention, at the request of the Lebanese President, to help in a crisis caused by political and religious tensions in the country. The crisis was over by the end of October that year and the foreign forces withdrew. It was reported that this was the first application of the Eisenhower Doctrine under which the US Government announced it would intervene to protect regimes it considered to be threatened by international communism.

"So far the enemy have taken one Jeep, two bazookas, and Ed's watch – Ed to shoot."

Daily Express, 18 July 1958

Sir Oswald Mosley, former leader of the British Union of Fascists, had attended a rally of the group in London's East End. As soon as he appeared, the crowd of several thousand demonstraters surged forward in protest and he was knocked to the ground.

"I caught your Leader a beauty with a tomato in 1936"

Sunday Express, 22 July 1962

Four days earlier, the lunar module "Eagle", from US spaceflight Apollo 11, landed the first two humans to walk on the Moon – Neil Armstrong and Buzz Aldrin

"I'm not having a son of mine christened Apollo and that's final."

Daily Express, 24 July 1969

Grandma's "regalia" was in honour of Charles and Diana's wedding which took place at St Paul's Cathedral three days after this cartoon appeared.

"You'll have to take it off Grandma – Butch doesn't like it!"

Sunday Express, 26 July 1981

94 This was the period of the "Kenyan Emergency" when Mau Mau groups fought to end Colonial rule. Kenya finalled achieved independence from British control on 12 December 1964.

"First time your father's smiled this holiday — when they told him he'd got to rejoin his regiment for Kenya."

Daily Express, 28 July 1960

Due to an extensive dock strike, the government declared a State of Emergency which empowered it to use servicemen to unload essential goods. At the same time, the long-standing daily issue of rum to sailors on duty on Royal Navy ships was stopped as a result of worries that alcohol could lead to unsteady hands when dealing with machinery.

"After you have informed them that they still may be doing Dock Duties in Liverpool remind them that after Friday there will be no more free issues of rum."

Daily Express, 30 July 1970

August

It had been revealed that Elizabeth Taylor was involved in an extramarital affair with Richard Burton, which started while they were making *Cleopatra*. Rex Harrison also appeared in the film. A few weeks earlier the Profumo scandal, involving Mandy Rice-Davies and Christine Keeler, forced John Profumo to resign as War Minister. The newspapers during this period carried a large number of photographs of those involved in these two sagas.

"First it was Liz Taylor, then it was you-know-who, then it was Mandy Rice-Davies, now we're back with Liz Taylor."

Daily Express, 1 August 1963

"You and your – 'Break strike and unload 'em for humane reasons!'"

Daily Express, 3 August 1972

"Is my chicken dressed O.K. to suit the colonel, sergeant?"

Sunday Express, 8 August 1954

Earlier that month, the British Government sent in two Special Air Service men into Gambia to reverse a coup and to rescue the family of the President who was in London attending the wedding of Prince Charles and Diana.

"George, do the SAS take on private rescue jobs?"

Sunday Express, 9 August 1981

100 Four days earlier, the Russians had succeeded in putting the manned Vostok 2 spacecraft into Space, piloted by Gherman Titov, for a full day. This was worrying for the USA as it represented a significant step forward for the Russians in the Space Race.

"Our Chief of Aeronautical Engineering says the Russian controlled Space Landing is a lot of 'malarkey' and he should know."

Daily Express, 10 August 1961

In 1958, the United States' President, Dwight Eisenhower, had hosted Queen Elizabeth's first visit to the USA as Queen. This cartoon refers to Eisenhower's visit to the UK the following year, which included a stay at the royal estate in Scotland. Perhaps the fact that the salmon fishing season had less than two months to go was the cause of the hostility.

"Watch your step, Hank. Hostile native down there – fishing."

Daily Express, 13 August 1959

102 In the early hours of 8 August that year, the Royal Mail train from London to Glasgow was stopped in Buckinghamshire and robbed. It became known as the "Great Train Robbery". The famous British criminal, Ronnie Biggs, was involved along with 14 other men but it was not reported that "boy Jack" was one of them.

"That you, sergeant? I don't know if there's any connection – but boy Jack's just treated the house the first time in forty years."

Daily Express, 15 August 1963

This was a period of rioting in London by anti-National Front groups including the International Marxist Group and the Workers Revolutionary Party, as well as the Social Workers Party featured here. Initially this complicated situation caused confusion for the police force having to deal with it.

"The note says: 'Thanks for doing our job for us'. Signed National Front Fascist Party."

Daily Express, 17 August 1977

A booming period for British farmers. Giles has located this cartoon at The Swan public house in Westerfield, just to the north of Ipswich, and a few miles from his farm at Witnesham.

"One article in the Press about British farming increasing its output by £249 million and it don't take this lot long to switch over from beer to Scotch."

Daily Express, 18 August 1966

Giles strongly disliked hooliganism in our national sport and spoke out against it through his cartoons on a number of occasions. This was a period when rioting by English football supporters in Europe led to the problem being called the "English Disease".

"The holiday in Spain did them good — got them in training for the start of football."

Daily Express, 19 August 1984

106 Following a period of major rioting, the British Army was deployed in Northern Ireland at the request of the Unionist Government. It was given the role of assisting the Royal Ulster Constabulary.

"Quiet, boys – it's the Army taken over from the cops."

Daily Express, 21 August 1969

The Notting Hill Carnival is an annual event held in London on August Bank Holiday Monday and the preceding Sunday. It takes place in the Royal Borough of Kensington and Chelsea and is organised by the British West Indian community. It is one of the world's largest street festivals.

"Hi, Dad – want to see some erotic Polaroids of you dancing at the Carnival before Mum sees them?"

Daily Express, 26 August 1980

For several months during 1967, violent clashes took place in Hong Kong between pro-Communist trade-unionists, protesting against British colonial rule, and the Hong Kong police force.

"Well now – all of a sudden our fervent discussion on Mao and Hong Kong comes to a peaceful close."

Sunday Express, 27 August 1967

At this time Britain was facing a sugar shortage due to a serious reduction in sugar cane imports from the Caribbean. The cane was going instead to more lucrative markets in the United States.

"My 2lb. sugar allocation I just signed for – it's gorn!"

Daily Express, 29 August 1974

September

The annual "Round the Island" yacht race coincided this year with the famous Isle of Wight Pop Festival.

"Horatio! You weren't watching the Round the Island Race at all. You were having a happening with those blasted hippies."

Daily Express, 2 September 1969

"If you can't beat 'em join 'em, as they say."

Sunday Express, 3 September 1972

Dame Naomi James was the first woman to sail single-handedly around the world (via Cape Hope) leaving Dartmouth, Devon on 9 September 1977 and finishing her voyage on 8 June 1978.

"With crews like mine, no wonder they sail round the world single-handed."

Daily Express, 5 September 1977

The National Council for Voluntary Organisations champions a wide range of voluntary sector bodies and produces reports on various issues relating to their responsibilities and works.

"This will put the NCVO report that Britain is a nation of Happy Families to the test – here comes Uncle Sidney and his happy breed."

Sunday Express, 9 September 1984

114 Britain was experiencing food shortages at this time which led to some people finding their own food sources. It is no coincidence that early in the following year, the hugely popular TV sitcom *The Good Life* appeared, in which characters, Tom and Barbara Good, attempted to produce all their own food on their smallholding, much to the amusement of their posh neighbours.

"Yes, I did read about the call for the nation to produce more food. Everybody out!"

Daily Express, 14 September 1974

This relates to the Ban the Bomb demonstrations which took place in London at this time and at which many thousands of demonstraters assembled in Trafalgar Square and elsewhere in London.

"Sidney, with a shortage of prison staff we think you're jolly rotten to sit down in sympathy with them."

Daily Express, 15 September 1961

116 The 1958 America's Cup was the first Cup match since 1937 and the first one to race in 12-metre class yachts as opposed to the larger J-class yachts used earlier. On this occasion, *Columbia* of the New York Yacht Club raced against the Royal Yacht Squadron's *Sceptre*. The Americans won 4–0.

"Which one are you rooting for, Bud?"

Daily Express, 18 September 1958

The Falklands War finished three months before this cartoon appeared. The human population of the Islands was less that 4,000 but it was estimated that its sheep numbered over half a million.

"Roger brought you a little present from the Falklands, Mummy, but he says that there was nothing in the shops."

Sunday Express, 19 September 1982

The Peace Conference being held at this time in the Swedish capital was aimed at achieving an improved level of worldwide arms control.

"How do they tie 'Bring us our bows, arrers, spears, chariots of fire' with the peace talks in Stockholm?"

Daily Express, 23 September 1986

This is an example of Giles combining a small news item (the desire of an individual to consider extreme measures in order to join the police force) with a nationwide issue (a very unpopular Act of Parliament) in a busy and confused crowd scene.

"I read this week that someone had himself stretched half an inch by an osteopath to make him tall enough to join the Police Force, but don't ask me why."

Sunday Express, 25 September 1960

This was a time when the whole country was gripped by a national scandal. A government white paper had just been issued, describing what was a major embarassment – the infamous Cambridge Four (later Five) Spy Ring in which a number of British academics had been unmasked as Russian spies.

"Look here, Sanders – are you watching me or am I watching you?"

Daily Express, 27 September 1955

"Great for our public image – the nick bunged full of drunk and disorderly birthday revellers."

Sunday Express, 30 September 1979

October

A new accord at this time pledged the USA to give economic and military aid to Spain in return for the Americans being able to use air and naval bases on Spanish territories.

"U.S.A. buys bases in Spain, hey ho...GILES"

Daily Express, 4 October 1953

The Japanese Emperor Hirohito was on a three-day state visit to London.

"It's not the first time the Hon. Son of Heaven has made me miss my lunch."

Daily Express, 5 October 1971

"Now you've taken up art, Charles, please pay special attention to the signature and avoid the same confusion as Constable and his son."

Sunday Express, 8 October 1978

The Labour Party Conference was held in Brighton the previous week at a difficult time for the Labour Government – the theme being "Britain in Crisis". The general public's attention was more taken by the news that Chi-Chi, the star attraction at London Zoo, was in Moscow, hopefully to mate with An-An – the giant panda there. In March 1965, Goldie, the Zoo's male golden eagle had caused a national sensation when he had escaped for 12 days whilst his keepers were cleaning out his cage. Obviously the Conservative Party felt in need of a similar distraction from its Conference.

"I know they all had Chi-Chi to take their minds off the Labour Conference – but I'm not letting Goldie out to take their minds off yours."

Sunday Express, 9 October 1966

126 There was some debate about ending complsory National Service at this time – but, in fact, it continued for another few years.

"Attention, please, gentlemen. The only cutting we're doing round here today is your 'air."

Daily Express, 11 October 1955

Harold Wilson was Prime Minister at this time and was obviously seeking to refresh his government.

"In his present mood for putting youth at the helm I don't like the look of this one little bit."

Daily Express, 14 October 1969

"I would urge that any bottle with a hammer & sickle label should be served to his Lordship with utmost caution."

Daily Express, 15 October 1985

The Minister of Education at this time was Sir David Eccles in Harold Macmillan's Conservative Government. Sir David, himself, went to the independent school Winchester College (which takes pupils from the age of 13 years) before going on to Oxford University. In this cartoon, Giles approached the idea with his own special brand of humour.

"The Minister of Education, urging that ALL children from five to eleven should be sent to State schools, said: 'Children of that age learning and playing together are not inhibited by any sense of differences'."

Daily Express, 17 October 1961

130　The Queen and Prince Philip, on a state visit to the USA, attended a banquet at the White House and a reception at the Waldorf Hotel in New York, shown here. The visit coincided with the 350th anniversary of the establishment of the first permanent English-speaking settlement in North America – Jamestown, Virginia.

"Elmer! I don't give a damn how pro-Monarchist you are – take it off and take it back where you rented it at once."

Sunday Express, 20 October 1957

The Cuban Crisis, caused by the USA's discovery of a Russian ship sailing towards Cuba with nuclear missiles aboard, resulted in a serious deterioration in relations between the Americans and the USSR at this time.

"Anglo-Am Relationship has sure gone way downhill when that one says 'no thanks'."

Daily Express, 25 October 1962

132   US cruise missiles arrived at the Greenham Common base in Britain at this time and were eventually removed in 1992. Police estimated that 200,000 people marched in London to protest against the deployment of these weapons in this country.

"Mrs Thatcher did have a word with the President about the inadvisability of parking it on your allotment but I guess the President told us to still go ahead."

Daily Express, 27 October 1983

Throughout 1963, the Beatles' popularity had been growing but their appearance at the London Palladium, two weeks before this cartoon was published, brought them to the attention of the national media. The media coined the phrase "Beatlemania" to describe the scenes of screaming fans wherever they appeared.

"I'm not dead – but I've got a ticket and I'll be killed in the rush if the others find out"

Daily Express, 29 October 1963

This was a difficult period in the country's economic situation with unemployment being recorded at over three million for the first time since the 1930s. Workers with a grievance would be able to take their case to a tribunal.

"I suggest a small increase in salary for Ivy might keep the Industrial Tribunal off our backs, M'Lady."

Sunday Express, 31 October 1982

November

The book *Lady Chatterley's Lover* caused a stir when it first became available in shops following a well-publicised obscenity court case. I am surprised that Grandma is not the first in the queue.

"All of a sudden we've become a literary-minded, puritanical, culture-seeking nation."

Daily Express, 3 November 1960

"Stand by for some real fireworks – Grandma's just found what's left of her hat you used on the guy"

Sunday Express, 6 November 1988

"Oh boy! Look what's marking us down at 25–1."

Sunday Express, 7 November 1971

A period when, due to a bakers' strike, there were severe bread shortages and, following panic buying, shops had to impose a bread rationing system.

"Even if you are getting fed up with lettuce leaves instead of butties, that's no way to talk about our bread strike Brothers."

Daily Express, 9 November 1978

The *Daily Express* Motor Rally with a fine view of Norwich Cathedral in the background. Giles loved motor sports and that could be Giles himself, as navigator, in his Jaguar XK120 in the bottom right-hand corner of the cartoon.

"They're wearing smog masks so that their navigators can't hear what they're calling 'em."

Daily Express, 11 November 1953

A pincer movement by Old Soldiers outmanoeuvring a younger member of the Senior Service.

"Two large Sommes, two large Ypres, one large Passchendaele, one large Nijmegen, £3.84."

Sunday Express, 13 November 1977

The Bank of England ceased issuing £1 notes at the end of 1984 and replaced them with the £1 coin – the note being finally removed from circulation in March 1988.

"What do ya mean 'What kept me?' – 100,000 £1 coins to the ton, that's what kept me!"

Daily Express, 15 November 1984

"Nah I expect you've all read that the Queen's going ter invite more ordinary people to the Palace in future..."

Sunday Express, 17 November 1957

"Be reasonable, Junior – Pa couldn't take all HIS little girl friends back to America when he went home after the war."

Sunday Express, 20 November 1960

The Suez Canal was closed by the Egyptians from early November that year to near the end of the following April. The Suez Canal Users Association was established to look after the interests of 15 countries who used the canal for shipping or trading purposes.

"Don't mind us – we're the Canal Users Association."

Sunday Express, 25 November 1956

The Local Government Act 1972, which introduced a major reform of local authorities in England and Wales, reducing the number of local authorities, had come into force in April. At this same time, economies in local government finances were being asked for. Perhaps a step towards breaking the unfair "glass ceiling", restricting women's advancement, was the main motive behind the management's decision.

"We have discussed democratically at great length the cutting down of our tea staff, and I fear it was a unanimous decision that Heads Miss Lovejoy stays."

Daily Express, 28 November 1974

146 A few days earlier, the government had devalued the pound in order to tackle the "root cause" of Britain's economic problems. Grandma's betting choices illustrate the scale of the unrest in the country at this time.

"Can his Granma have 6-4 the Rail Strike's on, 100-1 the Dock Strike's off, 60-1 the Bank Strike's on, 100-1 the School Strike's off and 6-4 the BOAC pilots..."

Daily Express, 30 November 1967

December

Smithfields Livestock Market in London was started in 1799. It moved to Earls Court in 1949 but was last held there in 2004. Maybe this was a period when London Underground was experiencinhg a high number of fare-dodgers. Maverick was a "cardsharper" character in a popular US Western show which appeared on British TV at this time.

"Oi! Just a minute, Maverick."

Daily Express, 5 December 1961

Four days earlier, the Amalgamated Engineering Union called a 24-hour strike over a dispute relating to wages. A fitter and turner in a yard in Hartlepool refused to obey and his fellow workers sent him to "Coventry". The dispute continued for some time. Giles loved capturing the general sense of confusion when a large group of children get together and this is a good example.

"Not in the widest sense, Wilkins, will I accept that Cinderella's Fairy Godmother was in any way an engineer."

Sunday Express, 6 December 1953

The Suez Canal Crisis began in July 1956 when President Nasser of Egypt nationalised the Canal. Early in the following November, Britain and France, in response, landed troops along the Canal. After pressure from the United Nations and others, the invading troops were withdrawn.

"Bought her a coffee in Port Said and she's followed me around ever since."

Sunday Express, 9 December 1956

150 This year, toys based upon the extremely popular *Star Wars* trilogy were being strongly promoted. This was also a period when it was reported that the USA had assembled a large stockpile of nuclear weapons as part of its aim for a Strategic Defense Shield.

"I've got to report to the Store Manager – a customer's complained that when she asked if we'd got any Star War games I said, 'No we aint – try the States'."

Daily Express, 10 December 1985

Mariner 2, the US robotic space probe to Venus, was launched on 27 August 1962 and passed by the planet on 14 December. Giles obviously decided to give this news item a seasonal theme.

"Receiving picture, sir, direct from Venus."

Sunday Express, 16 December 1962

This bread shortage was a result of strike action by bakery workers in Oxfordshire. Long queues formed outside bakeries and panic buying ocurred.

"I assure you the fact that I haven't got a thing in the place to sell you has nothing to do with your husband being my bread supplier."

Sunday Express, 18 December 1977

This was the first Christmas after the Road Traffic Act, 1967, which introduced a maximum legal blood alcohol level for driving in the UK.

"Keep laughing, buddy boy – I'll do mine in the morning when I'll be the only one who hasn't kissed the chairman of the board under the mistletoe..."

Daily Express, 21 December 1967

Bonnie Elizabeth Parker and Clyde Chestnut Barrow were US criminals during the period of the Great Depression. Their crimes involved robbing people and even killing when facing capture. They became well-known in this country through the film *Bonnie and Clyde* which was based upon their exploits.

"I think they heard you say they'd make a better Bonnie & Clyde, Vicar."

Sunday Express, 22 December 1985

"I've just had a happy Christmas thought – I forgot to get Auntie Vi's present."

Daily Express, 23 December 1972

156 This is Giles's contribution to marking the spirit of Christmas festivities after the opening of the first stretch of motorway in England. The Preston bypass, in Lancashire, was opened three weeks before this cartoon appeared. The first full-length motorway, the M1, was opened the following year.

Daily Express, 24 December 1959

The Cold War had entered a very dangerous stage and US politicians warned of the dangers of Soviet advances in technology and science, speculating that the Russians might possess superior missile stockpiles.

"We've had talks at top level and we've decided we're going to blast you off the face of the earth."

Daily Express, 27 December 1957

"One person who's not going to think much of it – my Aunty Bertha – that's certain."

Daily Express, 29 December 1964

"Just two more days of the Year of the Child then the Year of the Adult takes over in this house."

Sunday Express, 30 December 1979

All the cartoons in this book were copied from material in Carl Giles' own private archive, a huge collection of artwork, ephemera and correspondence, which is held by the British Cartoon Archive at the University of Kent. Carl Giles had been cartoonist for Lord Beaverbrook's *Daily* and *Sunday Express* for almost 20 years, when on 20 March 1962 the Conservative MP Sir Martin Lindsay tabled a motion deploring "the conduct of Lord Beaverbrook in authorizing over the last few years in the newspapers controlled by him more than 70 adverse comments on members of the royal family who have no means of replying".

Lindsay was wrong about the royal family having no means of reply. That day Prince Philip also vented his anger at Beaverbrook's campaign, during a press reception at the British Embassy in Rio de Janeiro. According to the paper's Brazil representative, the Prince declared that,, "The *Daily Express* is a bloody awful newspaper. It is full of lies, scandal and imagination. It is a vicious paper."

When the *Daily Express* reported this the next day, Giles decided to treat it as a joke. He knew the royal family enjoyed his cartoons; they often asked for the artwork. This had begun in 1948, when Prince Philip was sent a cartoon on the State Opening of Parliament, and over the next few years Giles received a steady stream of requests from Buckingham Palace for original drawings.

Giles drew the diminutive Lord Beaverbrook being escorted through the Traitor's Gate at the Tower of London, with a headsman's axe and block standing ready in the background. The caption repeated Prince Philip's condemnation of the *Daily Express*, but added laconically: "'Ah well,' said Lord B., as they trotted him off to the Tower, 'at least he takes it or he wouldn't know it was a bloody awful newspaper.'"

This was a brilliant response, which did much to defuse the situation. When Giles's cartoon was printed the next day, *Daily Express* staff were surprised to receive a phone call from the Queen's press secretary, with a message for Giles that "Her Majesty requests today's cartoon to commemorate one of her husband's most glorious indiscretions."

Giles sent off the artwork and in May 1962 found himself invited to "a small informal luncheon party" at Buckingham Palace with the Queen and Prince Philip. "I was filled with absolute dread," Giles recalled afterwards. "But as soon as she started to talk I was put at my ease…There were about half a dozen corgis running about in a completely uncontrolled state. Suddenly the Queen shouted, 'HEP'. It was like a bark from a sergeant major. The corgis immediately stood to attention. Then filed out of the room."

After the lunch Giles mischievously drew a cartoon of the guests leaving with corgi-savaged trousers. He sent it to the Queen, who returned her thanks through one of her private secretaries, noting that she was "glad that you got away without having lost, at least to the best of her knowledge, so much as a shred of your trousers".

After that Giles became what one *Daily Express* journalist called "a kind of cartooning jester to the royal family". By the time he retired in 1991 the royal family had more than 40 of his original drawings, the largest number being owned by Prince Philip, who shared Giles's anarchic view of the world.

The British Cartoon Archive, based at the University of Kent's Templeman Library in Canterbury, is dedicated to the history of British cartooning over the last two hundred years. It holds the artwork for more than 150,000 British political and social-comment cartoons, plus large collections of comic strips, newspaper cuttings, books and magazines. Its website at www.cartoons.ac.uk has over 200,000 cartoon images, including the majority of Carl Giles's published work.

Left: The cover of the 43rd Giles Annual, with evidence of yet another of Grandma's sisters.